52-WEEK INTENTION JOURNAL

52-WEEK INTENTION JOURNAL

Guided Prompts to Build
a Practice of Reflection, Focus,
and Meaningful Change

LAUREN BLANCHARD ZALEWSKI

ROCKRIDGE
PRESS

For general information on our other products and services or to obtain technical support, please contact our Customer Care Department within the United States at (866) 744-2665, or outside the United States at (510) 253-0500.

Rockridge Press publishes its books in a variety of electronic and print formats. Some content that appears in print may not be available in electronic books, and vice versa.

Interior and Cover Designer: Jennifer Hsu
Art Producer: Maya Melenchuk
Editor: Brian Sweeting
Production Editor: Dylan Julian
Production Manager: David Zapanta

Author photo courtesy of Dorothy Salvatori Photography

Paperback ISBN: 978-1-63807-886-9

R0

THIS JOURNAL BELONGS TO

INTRODUCTION

Welcome to the first day of the rest of your life! You've made the decision to live a life of inspiration, purpose, and intention, and I'm excited to walk alongside you on this journey toward your most wholehearted and joyful self. Throughout this journal, you'll learn to unlock the tools you need to live the life of your dreams and become an active participant in your own story. With the help of the weekly lessons contained in this journal, you'll design and take part in the life *you* want, on *your* terms. You have all the keys to unlock these tools inside you already, but you may not know how to find and apply them. I'll take you step-by-step through this process. You'll take control of the narrative of your life, applying it toward living mindfully, authentically, and intentionally, while enjoying it every step of the way.

A decade ago, I found myself at a crossroads. For years I lived with a chronic condition that caused me extreme pain. I allowed my struggle to take over every aspect of my life, and I turned to very unhealthy habits to deal with it. I eventually found myself in a place of darkness and despair while developing a serious dependence on alcohol. Instead of putting in the work to make the most of the cards I'd been dealt, I numbed myself. In the process, I lost my sense of purpose, my sense of self, and my lust for life.

Today, I'm very happily free from the bondage of those destructive habits and the emotional incarceration they helped create. Although I still struggle with chronic pain, I began a community on Facebook in 2015 called Attitude of Gratitude with Chronic Pain. We have more than 8,000 members, all of whom strive to live lives of gratitude, meaning, connection, and intention, despite our challenges.

The weekly lessons in this journal are the exact same tools I used in my own journey to create the life I have today, and they're also what we use in the Facebook community. Each morning, we start by stating our daily intentions. This habit has become a lifeline for many community members and is an important staple of our day. Intentions help us map out a loose vision for ourselves while embracing self-compassion and the ability to tweak things as we go along.

I sit here now writing my third book and also running a successful online community that brings my life incredible meaning and joy. I host a weekly live broadcast that helps others live their best lives despite their struggles, and I do so while living with chronic pain. I can tell you firsthand that if you're truly committed to this process, you can live the life you want and find exquisite meaning and joy. Life is not one-size-fits-all, and your life is *yours* to live. By setting forth on this journey and using this journal, you're being active in envisioning and writing the happily-ever-after part of your story. You'll make your life your own—and you'll *own* it proudly!

LIVING WITH INTENTION

Living with intention means ridding ourselves of the autopilot setting we often find ourselves on (especially when we're busy) and making a commitment to embrace a more mindful and balanced life. This manual setting is a more hands-on approach and centers on living intentionally and with awareness. It requires you to check in with yourself throughout the day to more clearly determine what's working well, as well as where you'd like to improve. Through this process, you can curate a life of inspiration and passion that leaves you excited to wake up each morning.

Many of us feel stuck in our lives and wish for more focus and joy. By letting go of old ways and living with intention, you can create, nurture, and participate in this vision you set out for yourself. When you give yourself permission to learn as you go along and start seeing setbacks as learning opportunities, you'll be amazed at how your life changes. You will soon find yourself crafting and nurturing the life of wholehearted joy and purpose you desire, without feelings of frustration and defeat—and you'll have fun doing it!

Perhaps you're in a career you don't enjoy and you're simply going through the motions each day. Or maybe you feel like you're in an endless slump, and you long to feel alive and exuberant. Through the practice of setting intentions, you'll discover and develop new passions and craft a life of meaning, happiness, and resilience.

An intentional life is a life of vision, focus, and joy. It gives you an awareness and the ability to see that vision clearly because you're fully and wholeheartedly awake.

By mixing things up a bit, you can flourish in your life. Flip the script on your own narrative. Along the way, you might even discover new passions, like I did when I began living intentionally. The life I live today seemed impossible to me a decade ago.

Making the decision to approach your life with intention is a monumental first step toward crafting the life you desire. Right now is the perfect time to start!

HOW TO USE THIS JOURNAL

This journal is a treasure trove of information that will help you find focus and meaning in your life through discovering and setting intentions. Making the decision to design a life of intention will allow you to reframe your mindset, helping you make positive changes to guide you on a journey toward joy and fulfillment. You'll be able to dig yourself out of the rut of day-to-day mindlessness and cultivate that soil to grow infinite possibilities for you to discover and develop.

By using this guided journal to plan the path toward the life you want to live, you'll reinforce what you truly desire by writing it down. Having goals or dreams in our minds and hearts is a wonderful thing, but the practice of writing them down cements those ideas. Your own writing will provide you with the road map you need to set out on this exciting new path. This journal will become your very own vision diary. It will enable you to tap into what you really want out of life, and how you'd like to find it.

Committing to the weekly practices is an important step in honoring this undertaking and gifting yourself the ability to craft the life you desire. This journal is not intended to be done sporadically or all at once. Instead, it's a weekly journey that I'll guide you through. Each week's topic is designed to follow what you worked on during the previous week. What you complete each week will unlock a new tool that will help you in the weeks that follow.

This journal is not a sprint; it's a marathon—but a fun one! By setting aside time at the beginning of each week, you'll find the most benefit from the exercises that we'll embark on together. By the end of the 52 weeks, you'll be well on your way to maintaining this life of intention that you diligently and mindfully worked on throughout the year.

Each week offers a different topic that I map out in detail in that week's reflections. I've chosen a powerful quote or affirmation to coordinate closely with each week's topic, bringing you the motivation and inspiration to embrace that week's idea. I've also provided you with prompts to go along with that week's reflection, which is where you'll apply the week's idea to your own life. You'll discover how it pertains to you and what you yearn to get out of it.

You've made an important first step by getting this book and committing to living the life you want. Grab your pen, and let's have fun designing your best life and finding out what sets your soul on fire!

LEANING IN AND SAYING YES TO LIFE

I can change the narrative of my story from surviving to thriving with some enthusiastic determination.

By making a commitment to living with intention, you're giving yourself an incredible gift and honoring yourself enough to be an active participant in your life. Rather than viewing life from the sidelines and mindlessly going through the motions of your day-to-day activities, you'll now approach this exciting undertaking of intention by leaning in and jumping in with both feet. Doing so requires adopting a *yes* mindset and ridding yourself of any self-doubt. When you take on a curious and enthusiastic attitude along with a belief in yourself, you erase your self-imposed limits and move toward the change you seek.

It can be difficult to lean in when you're hyper-focused on things you've tried in the past without much success. Erase those thoughts from your mind. They'll hold you hostage and prevent you from moving forward. Through this process, you'll dive into what excites you and makes you feel alive. You'll come to recognize what your strengths are and how you can capitalize on them. Learning from past experiences is an important part of your growth, but not giving it a shot just because you haven't yet found the life you're longing for is a roadblock you don't need.

Coming from a place of *yes* will get you on the right path toward an intentional life. What are some things you say no to that you can flip to a yes to help yourself move forward?

What has prevented you from saying yes to these things in the past?

Changing our view of ourselves from surviving to thriving is a way to get past our insecurities or unsuccessful endeavors. How are you a thriver in your life today as compared to a year ago?

How can you approach your day with more enthusiasm? "I am excited for this day" is a great mantra to repeat to yourself when self-doubt creeps in. Write another affirmation that can help you.

FINDING YOUR IKIGAI

I have value in this life and deserve to seek out things that bring me joy.

Being flexible, curious, and open to exploring new things will allow you to find your true passion and your reason for waking up in the morning. In Japanese culture, this concept is called *ikigai*, and it has long been believed to be a secret to living a long and happy life. It loosely translates to "life's purpose" or "reason for living." It's what gets you out of bed and puts you in a flow state. Ikigai looks different for everyone and is very specific. Perhaps you love volunteering at your local animal shelter or can spend hours working in your garden. Finding your purpose can lead to lifelong joy in body, mind, and spirit.

For most of my life, I envied people who love what they do and are great at it. I was always good at many things, but never great at any one thing. I discovered that when I took chances, tried new things, and took baby steps out of my comfort zone, I was able to find my ikigai—and it's nothing I could have imagined.

You're never too old to find your ikigai, and you never know what will end up finding you.

We can find great joy in activities that we never would have considered possible. What is something you've always wanted to learn how to do but felt was impossible?

If money, time, education, and resources were at your disposal, would it still seem impossible?

What are your personality traits or strengths that would aid you in making this dream a reality? What would your closest friends say you'd be great at?

What activities can you lose yourself in for hours on end?

CREATING YOUR SACRED SPACE

I will work toward creating and maintaining a sacred space that is mine alone. My creative energies and abundance will flow through here in order for me to pursue the life I desire.

This week, you'll create a special sacred space that is yours and yours alone. This space is where your abundance will flow. It doesn't have to be a whole room; the corner of a room can serve as this intention space. If a corner isn't possible, collect things such as art that makes you happy, quotes that inspire you, a plant, or photos, and keep them in a nice box. You can set up a temporary sacred workspace to use, and then put away the items when you're done.

You want this space to be welcoming and inviting, and maintaining an inspirational and uplifting space will encourage you to return to it regularly and continue toward your goals. Include your favorite colors, and if you have room, consider adding a small rug. I keep a battery-operated candle lit at all times in my special space. It signals to me that this area is serene and soothing, and I can use it to uncover my dreams and work toward them each day.

Keeping your space both physically and virtually decluttered will invite you to spend time there and remain focused and inspired.

Describe what your sacred space will look like. Where will it be? Consider such elements as art, bright colors, natural light—whatever makes it yours.

What can you add to the space to make it special? Buying a small plant or hanging up motivational quotes might brighten up the space.

How do you think having your own special space will benefit you? Can you think of a strategy to help you commit to keeping this space designated for you and your dreams?

What approach can you take to keep this space uncluttered so you can focus on your intentions? If necessary, make your space portable by keeping a box of your special things; you can easily set up and take down your space regularly, as needed.

OVERCOMING YOUR FEARS/ BELIEVING IN YOURSELF

You gain strength, courage, and confidence by every experience in which you really stop to look fear in the face . . . You must do the thing you think you cannot do.

—ELEANOR ROOSEVELT

It's natural to have some fear and trepidation when you're starting something new and different. Comfort zones are just so, well, comfortable, and stepping outside them can cause you to feel anxious or worried. Perhaps you've tried new ways of approaching your life, but they didn't go well or last very long.

We can talk ourselves out of succeeding by having negative thoughts, such as "I'm too old to start over" or "I'll never be able to do this." By leaning into our journey, believing in ourselves, and granting ourselves the permission to succeed, we can change our inner dialogue from one of fear to one of fearlessness.

Confidence doesn't come easily to a lot of people. Stepping outside your comfort zone may require a giant leap of faith—but you'll be glad you did it. The best blessings and rewards in life do not lie within our comfort zones, but outside the box we create for ourselves. It's up to us to want this life so much that we're willing to step outside that box.

Allowing fear to dominate our thoughts can prevent us from moving forward toward success. If failure was not an option, what would you do? List five things.

When has fear held you back from doing something you dreamed of?

Becoming our own biggest fan is a great step to creating the life we desire. In which areas of your life are you confident? Where are you more fearful? What do others say your strengths are?

Describe a time when you tried something that frightened you, but it worked out to be a big win.

BLOOM WHERE YOU'RE PLANTED

*There is nothing holding me back from starting today
on my journey toward a life of joy and intention.
The best time is now.*

Waiting to move toward your dreams until specific circumstances arise will leave you in a never-ending cycle of "someday," which will likely never come. Making a career change or starting that new diet only when you feel conditions are perfect will result in delaying the life you deserve to live. You can begin today by making that decision—and by working through this journal, you're off to a good start!

When have you ever heard anyone say they're in a perfect space in their life to spark change? Probably never! Situations are never ideal for positive change, so it's up to us to fertilize the ground we're already standing on. When we live with intention, we can beautifully bloom no matter where we are. Tomorrow is not promised, and putting off what we can start today robs us of a potentially meaningful and beautiful life.

Continuing to focus on what you want to accomplish is a great way to get motivated and stay the course. By carefully planning your intentions and visualizing the life of purpose you know you can achieve, you can bloom exactly where you're planted—right here, right now.

Visual aids, such as a vision board or scrapbook, can help us keep our intentions real and tangible. Keeping your desired life of intention and purpose in mind, what would you add to your vision board?

What challenges in your life have been holding you back until now?

We often tell ourselves things that make our end goals seem impossible when they really aren't. What untruths have you told yourself over the years that may have prevented you from moving forward?

What can you do differently today to bloom exactly where you're planted and ensure your desired success?

FINDING OUT WHO YOU ARE AND WHO YOU WANT TO BE

At the center of your being you have the answer; you know who you are and you know what you want.

—M. J. RYAN

In addition to considering your talents, gifts, and dreams, identifying your core values is an important aspect of living intentionally and finding your life's purpose. What you believe, how you live your life, how you were raised, and many other factors play into what makes you *you*.

Remaining true to yourself is an essential aspect of walking this journey in the most wholehearted way possible. Pretending to be someone you're not is pointless; you will eventually lose interest and resent yourself for not staying true to your beliefs. Being authentic and living your values to the best of your ability is the only way to enjoy the process and stand any chance of sticking with it in the long run. Otherwise, you'll just be going through the motions and not living life true to who you are.

This life is yours and doesn't belong to anyone else. You are the master craftsman, artist, and writer who creates, narrates, and lives your story—and it's up to you to write it.

Learning what your values are evolves over the course of your lifetime. Describe one of your core values that's nonnegotiable. Why is this core value nonnegotiable?

Have you ever had to go against your core values? How did it make you feel?

How have your values changed over the last 10 years? Explain why, and be as specific as possible.

List some of the strengths you embody because of your values and beliefs.

EMBRACING A GROWTH MINDSET/BEING FLEXIBLE

When I put my mind toward something I'm passionate about, learning is fun. I will embrace all knowledge that will foster my desire for growth.

One of the most exciting and fun aspects of living a life of intention is that you get to keep learning. I often call myself a lifelong learner. By allowing myself to be flexible and adaptable, I shine even brighter because I'm forever a work in progress. When you do your best while embracing a growth mindset, you'll be unstoppable. You do, however, need to let yourself encounter stumbling blocks along the way. These obstacles are how we truly learn; mistakes are simply stepping-stones on the way to your path of finding your true purpose and passion.

Be patient with yourself. As the saying goes, "Rome wasn't built in a day." We don't become experts in something as soon as we decide to learn about it. When you embrace a growth mindset without high expectations, you'll educate yourself and have fun trying to figure out what you love and what makes you *you*. When you approach each day with a hunger for knowledge, you become more curious about your life—and your personal possibilities will be endless.

Learn through the example of those who came before you, but don't limit yourself to what they did or are doing. Color outside the lines to make your path *your* path.

Endless resources are available for you to learn more about your passions or any topics that interest you. What are some of your favorite ways to educate yourself?

Is there someone whose work you'd like to learn more about? Perhaps you admire or are inspired by a particular author or artist. How can you go about accessing their work?

What is a skill you're expert in that you can teach someone else?

How might you apply this skill to living a life of intention?

HOLDING SPACE FOR OTHERS

> Lead by listening—to be a good leader you have
> to be a great listener.
>
> —RICHARD BRANSON

Part of living an intentional life is not only valuing your own time, but also showing others that you value theirs. When you're immersed in a conversation with someone, set aside other distractions and give them your full attention. This practice is known as holding space. It shows respect and tells others you value what they have to share. When we give listening ears and an open heart to others, we provide them with a safe space to share their truth. In turn, we hope to be given the same opportunity. We can listen without judgment and without feeling the need to offer solutions or opinions—unless asked. This thoughtful act of mindful listening earns trust and respect from those we care about.

Chances are, you know someone who isn't the best listener. You can be deep in a discussion with them, but you can tell they're not giving you their full attention. This experience can be very frustrating. They may not mean any disrespect, but their behavior conveys that what you have to say isn't worthy of their attention. We can avoid giving this impression by maintaining eye contact, nodding when appropriate, and showing others we deserve and appreciate this trust they have gifted us.

Listening without judgment can be difficult because we want to offer solutions or suggestions when someone shares with us. How difficult is it for you to just listen without wanting to respond? Why?

Describe a time you offered unsolicited advice and it wasn't met with gratitude. How could this situation have been different if you hadn't offered your opinion?

Asking questions, looking directly at the other person, and responding to their vulnerability are all habits that develop trust. In what ways are you a good listener? What can you do to develop better listening skills?

Describe a time when someone shared something deeply personal and authentic with you. How did you feel afterward? Can you recognize why they trusted you?

PACING YOURSELF

I am determined to live with intention and commit to taking baby steps to ensure long-standing success toward my life of joy and purpose.

In years past, I'd often find something new that interested me and go a bit overboard. I'd read everything I could find on the subject and purchase lots of supplies. I'd always have the best of intentions going in, but because I went full tilt and skipped the important step of intentionally mapping out my process, I'd eventually lose steam. It was a stage, not a way of life.

Living our best life with intention is a process. It takes time to ease into it. Making the time to determine, in detail, what you want out of your life will gift you with a mapped-out vision and a solid plan going forward. This plan will ensure that your way of life fuels your passion and taps into your ikigai.

At the end of each year, I encourage my members to set New Year's *intentions,* which is a more sustainable and successful approach than making resolutions, which often involve implementing drastic changes overnight. By educating yourself on living mindfully through intention, you can make significant positive changes in your life that will gift you with an enduring lifestyle.

Having an accountability buddy can help you achieve positive changes and live mindfully and intentionally. Who could you ask to support you on this journey? Why did this person come to mind?

How can you ensure that you take things slowly while maintaining determination to carry out your plans? An example is writing out a plan on paper.

Studies show that only about 8 percent of people who make New Year's resolutions follow through with them. What resolutions have you made that eventually fizzled out? Why do you think they didn't work over the long term?

What is your biggest motivation to commit to your success for the long haul?

CHANGING YOUR NARRATIVE

I can change the course of my day by viewing tasks as opportunities. I will remember that these are tasks I get to do, not tasks I have to do.

Changing the way you view your intentional actions, tasks, and goals can make all the difference in how you feel about pursuing them. Rather than looking at these tasks as things you *have* to do, look at them as things you *get* to do. It flips the script of your thoughts to abundance and gratitude rather than exhaustion and anxiety.

Think about all the things you set out to do each day, such as making phone calls or returning a library book. Now look at them through the lens of being told you have only a few months to live. Do you still think of them as burdens, or do you now see them as privileges?

Throughout this journal, you're working diligently to craft and implement this new life of intention. You're actively pursuing a life of meaning, taking a more mindful approach to your life. By embracing this new narrative of "I get to," you'll tie it all together, ensuring your own success as you move toward the life of your dreams. Your life is a privilege you get to take part in—right now!

Looking at the day with the idea that we *must* do things can create unnecessary stress and anxiety. How has this sort of thinking been an issue for you?

Think about how you organize your daily tasks. How can you make them both manageable and enjoyable? (Note: Having a lengthy to-do list can lead to procrastination.)

Make a to-do list of five things, writing "I have to" in front of each. Then cross out "I have to" and write "I get to." How does this process change your thinking?

Describe three creative ways you can remind yourself to change your narrative. Copy each onto a sticky note and keep them in view in your sacred space.

INSPIRATION

Surround yourself with people who are only going to lift you higher.

—OPRAH WINFREY

Finding inspiration is one of the most important tools I use to live my best life of intention. Without the motivation to keep on keeping on and feeling inspired by others, we would be left with silence when answering the question "What's the point?"

Other people often inspire us to keep moving forward. Maybe you admire a guru you've never met or you strive to be like someone you're close to. Using these sources of inspiration can be of great benefit. When you see someone who embodies your values, note what they actually do. Make sure they walk the walk. Anyone can offer inspiring words, but do they practice what they preach? Paying attention can be the key to finding the inspiration you need.

On my toughest days, reading inspirational quotes can give me that extra boost I need. Joining a community of like-minded people who inspire you is another powerful way to stay the course and continue on your journey toward intention.

Write about how you've grown since starting this journal. It will be inspiring to look back and see how far you've come.

What would your friends say is the most inspiring thing about you? Do you agree with them?

Whom do you find inspiring? Describe what you like about this person, and specify ways you can emulate them.

What words, actions, or people inspire you? How about a movie, book, or quote? Write your favorite inspirational quote and refer to it when you need a dose of daily inspiration.

ALLOWING YOURSELF TO DREAM

*I am limitless and will not conform to anyone else's ideas
of who I am. I am capable of great things!*

Having dreams is beautiful, and dreams are not just for children. When you settle, you compromise your worth by accepting less than what you truly desire. Thinking outside your comfort zone and without limits gives you the space you need to grow to your full potential. I used to believe that the older I got, the less likely it was that I'd do the things I had dreamed about. As time ticked away, I told myself that if I'd hadn't reached my dreams or found my passion by that point, seeking them was pointless.

I was wrong. As of this writing I am in my early 50s, and I am only just beginning to feel my life's purpose and live a life of passion and meaning. By opening my eyes to life and allowing myself to venture, step-by-step, past the boundaries of my comfort zone, I have uncovered my reason for waking up in the morning and what blissfully puts me into a state of flow. It was unfathomable only a few years ago.

Your dreams are yours and yours alone, and you have the power to make them a reality. Don't let anyone tell you differently.

Dreams may seem far-fetched, but they're behind many great success stories throughout history. Think of someone who achieved a dream they'd always strived toward. How does this inspire you?

What qualities helped this person reach their goal? Do you have, or would you like to have, similar qualities?

Think of a dream you've had since you were a child. How can you take that first step into making it a reality?

List three strengths that can help you reach your dream.

AFFIRMATIONS/MANTRAS

Today I am blessed.

—MAYA ANGELOU

An affirmation is positive thinking paired with self-empowerment. Affirmations are positive statements that help you overcome and offset any negative self-talk you may be tempted to engage in. The way we speak to ourselves makes a huge difference, and often we don't realize it. I use positive self-talk daily. It may feel a bit funny at first, but it provides a powerful punch toward attaining the life we desire.

Since embarking on living my life with intention a decade ago, one of the tools I have sworn by is stating affirmations. Saying them out loud contributes to their power. A study published in *Social Cognitive and Affective Neuroscience* showed that stating affirmations can decrease stress, increase well-being, improve academic performance, and open people to changing their behaviors and habits.

Each day when I get out of the shower, I tell myself, "Good girl!" because showers can often be challenging when you live with chronic pain. I'm my own personal trainer of sorts, reinforcing this behavior. Affirmations help you follow through on actions and turn negative thoughts into powerful ones. Mantras like "I am ready to live my best life and approach each day with a positive attitude!" can serve as personal mission statements for achieving what you want out of life.

Changing your dialogue to saying yes and expressing self-compassion will produce a better long-term outcome. Describe your regular inner dialogue. If you tend to speak to yourself in a negative voice, how can you change it?

Repeat these affirmations: "I am worthy." "I am capable of great things." "I am focused on a life of positivity." "I am grateful." How do you feel when you say them out loud?

Writing your own personal mantra can be helpful toward creating your life of intention. Craft a mantra for yourself and write it down. Place it somewhere you can see it when you need a boost.

YouTube has many great videos with helpful affirmations. I do mine in the morning. Write down some books or websites that offer affirmation ideas (earmark this page to reference when you need it).

ACCEPTANCE AND LETTING GO

One of the happiest moments in life is when you find the courage to let go of what you can't change.

—ANONYMOUS

When I embarked on this new life of intention—I call it "Lauren 2.0"—almost a decade ago, I had to learn and accept what I could control and what I couldn't. It was a really tough lesson because I often wanted to control the outcomes of situations or fix people or circumstances that I didn't like. Accepting conditions as they are is one of the most important and valuable principles I apply to my life today.

As I grew more aware of what I couldn't control, I learned the incredible value of letting go of problems that aren't mine to solve. Refraining from trying to control the actions or words of others around me or from attempting to fix the unfixable has given me a sense of peace and renewed energy, allowing me to concentrate on what I *can* control.

Taking a good, clear look at your life and identifying what you can release will enable you to move forward with grace, accepting what you can't change and focusing with intention on the things you can. Journaling regularly on this topic is a great way to release frustrations, and it will also help you identify more easily what you can't change.

Make a list of aspects of your life you consider unsatisfactory. Next to each item, note whether you can control it. How might you benefit from accepting what is beyond your control?

What about this list surprised you? Maybe you discovered that more situations are beyond your control than within it. What benefits might come from this discovery?

Trying to fix others can create a vicious circle that leaves us feeling resentful and frustrated. If you're doing it, describe the dynamic. How can you break this habit? What benefits do you imagine?

Write down your frustrations from this week, noting what you can control versus what you can't. Then write an affirmation that will help you remember to let go.

A POSITIVE ATTITUDE WINS EVERY TIME

I have the power to choose my level of happiness and release all negativity from my life.

The writing and work I do through my online community revolve around one general mission: accepting our situations as they are at any moment, recognizing what we can and can't control, and using what's in our tool kit to create the life we desire. In my many years of working directly with people who live with chronic physical and/or emotional pain, I have seen firsthand how essential it is to approach our situations with a positive attitude if we wish to move forward on a journey toward light and wholehearted joy.

It's not a simple fix of mind over matter, of course. When things aren't going well, it's difficult to look on the bright side and move forward toward the life you desire. It requires hard work, determination, and, perhaps most important, a willingness to look at the abundance in your life and embrace gratitude.

Think about the people in your life who inspire you. Ask yourself whether they have an attitude of gratitude or concentrate mainly on what's lacking in their lives. The people I admire and gravitate toward almost always come from a place of positivity and abundance. It's contagious.

Think of someone you look up to who has successfully handled a challenging situation. Describe their approach. Why did this person and situation come to mind?

What three lessons can you take from this example to apply to your own life? Does considering this situation inspire an attitude shift toward the positive?

Describe a time when your attitude had a direct effect on a situation's outcome (like a squabble involving family or friends or a work situation). What happened and how did you deal with it?

We can make a conscious decision to be happy each day as we wake up. What tools can you use first thing in the morning to boost your mood? Some examples are music and affirmations.

LAUGHTER AND FUN

We don't stop playing because we grow old;
we grow old because we stop playing.

—GEORGE BERNARD SHAW

Having structure throughout the day helps us live in the moment mindfully and be an active participant in all aspects of our day. Of course, it doesn't mean we shouldn't have fun. Laughter is a welcome part of life that can improve our mood by acting as a release valve for stress and anxiety.

I live with a chronic illness, and I used to take myself a bit too seriously. Our struggles in life are nothing to laugh at, but they also shouldn't keep us from enjoying life, including laughing and having fun. Allowing ourselves to laugh is not an admission that we don't have struggles; it simply means we love our life more than we hate our pain.

Laughter brings a plethora of health benefits, whether you're laughing at a sitcom, with a friend, or at yourself. Studies show that in addition to stress reduction, laughter boosts our immune system and even relieves pain. The rise and fall of our heart rate when we're having a good laugh provides a welcome release from tension, allowing us to look at life a bit differently—without being so serious.

Have fun! It will help you fall in love with your life.

Humor can be learned. If you feel you lack a sense of humor, the good news is you can develop it. Describe some things that make you laugh.

How do you feel physically after having a good laugh? How about emotionally?

Think about a time when laughter eased tension in your life. What were the circumstances? How did you feel afterward?

Make a list of physical objects that make you laugh, like greeting cards, jokes, articles, or token items. Bring them into your sacred space as a reminder not to take yourself too seriously.

SETTING ATTAINABLE GOALS

Our goals can be reached only through the vehicle of a plan, in which we must fervently believe, and upon which we must vigorously act. There is no other route to success.

—PABLO PICASSO

Setting forth on any new path is exciting, and no doubt this new life of intention is something you're focused on achieving. Although we should never stop shooting for the stars, the majority of our intentions need to be realistic. It certainly doesn't mean you shouldn't stretch yourself or go outside your comfort zone, but try to avoid setting yourself up for failure. Make sure most of your goals are attainable.

Establishing clear milestones along your journey will allow you to meet your goals and celebrate them as you go. When you set these goals, make sure they're concise and measurable.

Part of having a growth mindset involves stretching ourselves, and we can't do so if we don't step outside our comfort zone a bit. Finding a balance between setting attainable goals and having a few long-shot dreams can achieve that happy medium of reaching for the stars while still setting yourself up for success.

Having clear, measurable goals will help you succeed. List some ways you can determine when you reach a milestone (such as time devoted to the goal or how many glasses of water you drank).

How do you feel when you reach a goal? How do you celebrate when you accomplish something? If you don't normally do so, how might you start?

Incentives such as enjoying play time on social media or taking snack breaks can help us stay on track toward our goals. What incentives can you offer yourself? Explain why each will help.

List a few tools you can use to track your goals (like productivity apps or a paper planner). Map out your desired milestones, tweaking them as needed.

PLANNING ON PAPER AND KEEPING TRACK

Paper is to write things down that we need to remember.
Our brains are used to think.

—ALBERT EINSTEIN

Many great productivity apps are available, but I'm a big believer in the power of writing things on paper. We don't have the mental bandwidth to handle everything on our plates. Planning our days and our intentions on paper provides many benefits for moving toward a life of joy and fulfillment. It's why this journal is so important.

I plan my day on paper—every day. The act of physically writing something down and then looking at it in my own handwriting serves as a memory boost. I do use some productivity apps, but pen and paper have served me much better. Planners, journals, whiteboards, and similar tools are also great for daily planning.

If you have only three things on your to-do list and you think you should be able to remember them, you may find yourself repeating these tasks on an endless loop in your mind. This habit will make the tasks feel a lot more arduous than they are. Writing down tasks frees up our brains to be more mindful and aids us in our quest toward our intended joy and purpose.

These days, our brains are overloaded with things to remember, including PINs, passwords, and tasks. Describe how you could benefit from mapping things out on paper.

This week, think about the best, simplest way for you to keep track of things and free up your mind for creativity. If you require more than this journal, what might you use?

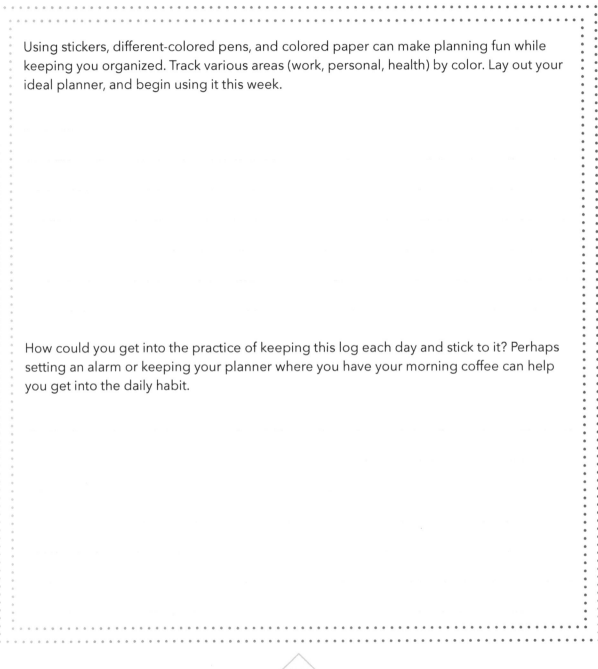

Using stickers, different-colored pens, and colored paper can make planning fun while keeping you organized. Track various areas (work, personal, health) by color. Lay out your ideal planner, and begin using it this week.

How could you get into the practice of keeping this log each day and stick to it? Perhaps setting an alarm or keeping your planner where you have your morning coffee can help you get into the daily habit.

TREATING YOURSELF

I will honor myself and my commitment by rewarding myself daily for sticking to my intentions, keeping things fresh and fun.

Being able to craft, grow, and set forth into an intentional life is a reward in itself. When you focus on mindfully walking toward a life of fulfillment and joy, the reward is in the journey, and you'll fall in love with your life every day. But as we've all experienced, some days just drag and we need a boost. At times like this, treating yourself can prove to be incredibly beneficial, keeping your process feeling fun and new.

Rewards aren't necessarily material. When you map out your timeline for the day, include some mindless fun, such as a 10-minute social media break or 30 minutes to catch your latest binge-watch pleasure on Netflix. Although the idea of setting intentions involves getting away from mindlessness, we also need to allow ourselves to turn off our brains for a little while. In my community, we call it "reboot" time for our emotional health.

Setting aside regular breaks from work will break up the day and keep things fresh.

Rewards throughout the day can keep us focused and goal-oriented. Write down some ideas for treats you can give yourself. What appeals to you?

Make a schedule for incorporating those rewards. Find a good balance between living with intention and essential break time.

Think of ways to keep yourself from spending too much time on mindless activities like social media (such as writing out a schedule or setting a timer). How can you reward yourself for limiting this downtime?

If you have feelings of guilt around rewarding yourself, write an affirmation as a reminder that treating yourself is essential self-care. Repeat it when feelings of guilt creep in.

BE PREPARED

*Give me six hours to chop down a tree and
I will spend the first four sharpening the axe.*

—ANONYMOUS

Educating yourself and being prepared for your journey are important to your commitment to yourself. By learning all you can about what you need to craft the life you desire, you're deciding to suit up and show up in order to do this fun and fulfilling work.

In addition to working through this journal, you may want to reach out to others who live a life similar to what you're envisioning. You might be surprised at how willing people are to help you along your journey and share with you how they accomplished their dreams, whether professional, spiritual, physical, or social.

Online communities are a wonderful resource, as are books that focus on various subjects. Learn as much as you can about your passion, and you'll find it becomes part of you. Eventually you will become the expert, helping the next person who reaches out for guidance.

I invite guests to my live weekly broadcast to provide their wisdom and insight into ways we can live our best life of intention and joy. I've had famous authors, therapists, and well-known names come on, and very rarely does anyone turn me down. You never know unless you try.

Describe several resources you can use to educate yourself about your passions and interests. The internet (especially Facebook groups) is an invaluable resource, as are magazines and books.

Create a list of 10 people—including people you know or even experts in the field—who embody something you value. What do these people have in common?

Send an email to one (or more) of these people. Explain why you want to talk to them and express appreciation for any help they can offer. Outline your message here.

How does your confidence level change when you are aptly prepared for something as opposed to when you're not?

STAYING TRUE TO YOUR WORD

Be impeccable with your word. Speak with integrity. Say only what you mean . . . Use the power of your word in the direction of truth and love.

—DON MIGUEL RUIZ

Honoring your word to others is an important part of mindfulness and a life of intention because it shows respect and commitment. Although life happens—and we need to allow for changes with flexibility and ease—doing our best to show up when we say we will indicates not only how much we value the other person, but also how much we value ourselves.

Our word says a lot about us and our beliefs. Being wishy-washy in our word will inevitably make us wishy-washy in life. Being adaptable to the ebbs and flows of life is important, but doing our best to stick to our word and honor our commitments to others shows that we respect them.

Using your voice to speak with integrity and kindness, as opposed to toxicity and gossip, shows your true colors. Keep this concept in mind when you choose your words toward others as well as yourself. Being a gossip is a surefire way to lose the trust and respect of those you love and value.

Keeping commitments when possible shows sincerity and respect to others. Describe how it feels when others flake out on you repeatedly. Why do you feel this way?

How could you learn from these feelings and use them as fuel to be truer to your own commitments?

How could you improve your commitment level while remaining flexible? Write a strong mantra to remind yourself what keeping your word means to you, such as "I stay true to my word because it shows respect and integrity."

When you're able to stop yourself from speaking negatively and contributing to gossip, how do you feel about yourself? Why?

BREAKING OLD HABITS

> You leave old habits behind by starting out with the thought,
> "I release the need for this in my life."
>
> —DR. WAYNE W. DYER

It can be difficult to break ourselves of old habits that may not be working well for us. We might not even recognize that some of our habits could be holding us back from the life we yearn for. Living with and setting intentions allows us to take a step back, look at our life through a new and objective lens, and recognize what isn't working. It may not be a bad habit per se, but an old behavior that no longer serves us on our quest toward a more mindful life. Maybe you spend too much time on social media, or you put things off until the last minute. If these habits don't serve you, you can be proactive in changing them.

Our comfort zones get awfully cozy and may keep us from wanting to make changes. As the saying goes, "Old habits die hard." These behaviors can become quite routine for us, but if the routine isn't working, it's time to change.

Partnering with a friend or loved one who understands your desire to quit the old behavior can be a great way to hold yourself accountable and push you toward this goal.

What is one habit you'd like to give up? Describe how you might go about making this change.

In what ways would your life improve if you dropped this habit?

Now think of a different habit you can replace the old one with in order to ease the transition. Describe this new habit and how it will benefit you on your journey.

What resources can give you a boost in dropping your bad habit? Add one, such as an online or in-person support group, to your tool kit this week and track your progress.

CREATING AND ESTABLISHING POSITIVE HABITS

I will commit to my growth by incorporating new ways of doing things into my life, and I will approach these changes with zest and determination.

Dropping old habits may require us to seek out new, healthier, more helpful ways of accomplishing things. If a bad habit was filling a need in our lives, replacing it with a positive one can fill that space while allowing us to move toward our true north.

Incorporating new ways of doing things can be uncomfortable at first. Getting past that initial discomfort will allow you to embrace these new habits, and planning alternative routes will help you move forward.

Choose new habits that will nurture you in mind, body, and spirit. Approaching changes from this angle will gift you with the room to grow toward the life you desire, and making these new habits fun and creative will keep you on track. A University College London study involving 96 participants indicates that it takes an average of 66 days for new habits to become established. Making your new habits enjoyable is important in establishing that new routine so you stick with it.

Giving ourselves permission to explore alternate ways of doing things is important to establishing good habits. What is one positive habit that you'd like to incorporate into your life? What benefits do you imagine?

Make a list of actions you can realistically take to see this new habit through and ensure your success.

How can you make this new habit enjoyable? Perhaps the social aspect of involving a good friend would make it fun.

How can you reward yourself for establishing this beneficial new habit?

FINDING YOUR COMMUNITY

Although I can do great things on my own, I recognize the importance of finding a reliable support system. I will work on establishing these relationships.

I am a huge proponent of being part of a community. The connections we make with others are good for us in so many ways, especially improving our emotional and even physical health. In my darkest days of rock bottom, I isolated myself and wouldn't even return text messages from friends. My head was a dark neighborhood I inhabited alone, and by separating myself from everyone, I began to feel unique in my feelings and thoughts—which was a major factor in my deterioration and prevented my growth.

Finding and building a support system is a beautiful gift, and so many options are available to us today to seek out like-minded people. Groups on social media have been created for just about any purpose and topic you may be passionate about. Meeting comrades with similar interests and passions can help us map our lives of intention, and we can find accountability partners to keep us focused on our path.

Although setting out on this journey on our own is wonderful, sharing it with another person or a group will give you that extra boost to keep you focused, inspired, and on track.

Finding kindred spirits and people who inspire us can bring enormous joy and resilience to our lives. What do you hope to find in a friend or community? What benefits do you envision?

Where could you go to find your community? Your town newsletter or Facebook groups might be options.

Connection and community is a two-way relationship that requires work to maintain. What are some qualities that make you a good friend? What characteristics do you seek out in others?

Think of someone in your life who supports your dreams and whom you trust to be an accountability partner. What about this person makes them come to mind?

THE ART OF THE UNPLUG

Almost everything will work again if you unplug it for a few minutes, including you.

—ANNE LAMOTT

Last summer, my kids were planning to join my husband and me on our first family vacation in many years. But when my daughter got sick, we decided not to go away. Instead of continuing to work, I treated myself to a staycation.

This occasion is when I learned the true beauty behind the art of the unplug. Until that point, I'd always made myself available to everybody 24/7. All day, every day, I'd hear beeps and alerts from texts and messaging apps. I hadn't realized those notifications were stressing me out, but when I disabled them I began to appreciate being unavailable at various times throughout the day.

Today, I incorporate the art of the unplug by making myself unavailable at certain times each day. With the exception of my family, everyone goes on mute, and I get to the messages when I decide to. By incorporating this approach, you can gift yourself serenity and the ability to focus on your intentions. It's a much more mindful way to work because it allows you to concentrate on one thing at a time. You may be surprised by how much more productive and less stressed you are when you unplug!

Think about how available you are to others on a daily basis. List a few ways you can give yourself, and your intentions, the focus you deserve.

This week, ease into disabling notifications throughout the day. Describe the difference this habit makes in your focus and mindset. What changes have you noticed by the end of the week?

How do you see your life changing if you're not constantly responding to emails and texts? How might creating this space in your day benefit you in your endeavors?

What is the worst thing you imagine happening if you're not available at all times? If you're not comfortable with this idea, how could you tweak it?

KEEP YOUR EYES ON THE PRIZE

I am capable of anything I set my mind to, and I am committed to achieving my desired life. I use mindfulness and the other tools in my tool kit to stay the course and be true to my abilities.

You will experience ebbs and flows in maintaining focus on and excitement about the intentional life you desire. Some days, you set out with pure enthusiasm, and other times, you may feel your routine is getting a bit tired. It's a natural progression through life; the excitement of the honeymoon period at the beginning of any new relationship or undertaking doesn't last forever.

A great way to maintain focus and keep your excitement level high is to mix things up throughout the day. Although it's important to maintain a schedule and stick to our intentions, we don't have to do it the same exact way every day. If you're a creature of habit and tend to do the same affirmations each day and follow the same or a similar routine, there's nothing wrong with keeping things fresh and trying something new. You might even like the new approach better and decide to go that route for a while!

Believing in your abilities and having self-compassion is a powerful combination that will enable you to maintain your focus. Keeping your end goal in mind will help get you over those hump days when your drive and energy may be somewhat diminished.

Having a clear vision for your future can help you stay the course toward the life you desire. Where do you want to be in five years? How do you see yourself?

Now look back on where you were five years ago. How did you arrive where you are today?

What tools can you use to remind yourself that you're capable of achieving the life you desire? Examples are a personal mantra, journaling, and following a gratitude practice.

Write a positive mantra for yourself to read daily that will help you stay focused and keep your eyes on the prize.

ONE THING AT A TIME

Multitasking divides your attention and leads
to confusion and weakened focus.

—DEEPAK CHOPRA

Many of us have convinced ourselves that we're proficient multitaskers, but research shows that we're actually less productive when we try to concentrate on too many things at once. Focusing on one task at a time allows us to do that one thing well, and then move on to the next without cluttering our brain.

Science shows that we're not actually capable of doing two things at once very well. I've never met anyone (including myself) who can talk on the phone and type an email at the same time. We might believe we're being efficient by multitasking, but what we're really doing is switching between tasks very quickly—and not giving either of them our full attention. Basically, there's no place for multitasking when you're living mindfully with intention.

Rather than trying to multitask, give yourself time frames to complete each task individually. Let's say you have three tasks that you want to complete in the next 30 minutes. Instead of doing them all simultaneously and putting your brain into unnecessary overdrive, take 10 minutes to do each. You'll do a better job, without feeling crazed in the process. Stepping back, slowing down, and breathing deeply can help us remember to focus on a single task.

When we try to perform several tasks at the same time, we're actually diluting the outcome of all those things. Where in your life do you try to do too many things at once?

List a few ways you can simplify your approach and focus on one thing at a time.

This week, try to keep your focus and be mindful while doing one thing at a time (it may take practice). Write down how you feel after each task.

How do you notice the quality of your work changes when you're mindful of staying focused on that one task? Describe a couple of examples.

SETTING BOUNDARIES

I will work toward recognizing my part in overextending myself, and honor my personal journey by establishing healthy boundaries and saying no when I need to.

Setting boundaries is difficult for many of us. We can work to rewire our brain, going from a default "yes to everyone else" setting to a healthy new option of "yes to me." Many of us are raised from a young age to help others at all costs; this habit can be detrimental to our well-being when we put everyone else ahead of ourselves. It also prevents us from being able to fully embody a growth mindset.

Setting healthy boundaries serves many purposes, including two major ones. First, it allows you to honor *your* needs, which you may have ignored until now. This practice is an example of setting new and positive habits for yourself. You're not obligated to be at the mercy of others. Take care of yourself—you are worthy and deserving of that. Second, many of us are afraid people won't like us anymore if we say no to them. What you'll find, though, is that you actually garner *more* respect from people when you establish and clearly share what you're willing to do and where you need to draw the line. Doing so shows assurance, self-confidence, and growth toward your true north.

In what areas do you have difficulty setting boundaries? Be specific.

Consider whether any relationships in your life might be keeping you from healthy growth. Maybe a family member or friend tends to take advantage of you. Briefly describe what is happening.

List some healthy boundaries you can establish for yourself, such as not scheduling anything during your designated "me" time or periodically saying no to someone you typically say yes to.

How do you believe your life would improve if you could stick to your own healthy boundaries successfully? List at least three ways.

MAKING CHOICES

> Don't ever make decisions based on fear. Make decisions based on hope and possibility!
>
> —MICHELLE OBAMA

It's estimated that the average adult makes more than 35,000 conscious decisions each day. We aren't mindful of most of them, but when tough choices come down the pike, they can paralyze us with worry, anxiety, and indecision. We can overthink our decisions to the point of numbing ourselves and then second-guess our choice after we've finally made it.

To be more mindful and intentional with your choices during the day, first determine the weight of that decision. Is the answer truly worth the time you're spending on it? Most of the time, you'll find that it isn't. By taking an objective look to determine the importance of the decision at hand, you can spend only the necessary time on it, and then move on.

In my work with my community, thousands of people rely on me, on a daily basis, to make a ton of decisions. I tell my team the same thing I tell myself: If you use your gut and your heart, you'll never make a wrong decision. And even if that choice doesn't lead to what you hoped for, if you go with your instincts and stay true to your answer, you'll never second-guess yourself.

Your heart and your gut will never steer you wrong. Describe a poor decision (or decisions) you've made. Do you feel that something stood in the way of you making a better choice? What?

Describe the circumstances around a decision you spent a lot of time making. Was the time expended worth the answer and outcome it generated? Why or why not?

By sticking with our final decision, we show confidence in ourselves. Think of someone you know who is wishy-washy about their choices. How does this tendency strike you?

How can you work on allotting the appropriate amount of time to your choices? What might help you better trust the decisions you make?

BUILDING RESILIENCE

I have tools at my disposal to rewire my brain toward resilience, and I will commit to these techniques to build my strength through times of struggle.

Resilience is the ability to cope with life's challenges, and our power lies in our ability to face and handle these struggles as they arise. Difficulties can range from everyday disappointments to traumatic events that are excruciatingly difficult to maneuver through. We all have tough times and experiences in our lives, and how we cope with them can make all the difference in our ability to move forward with intention and joy.

We can do many things to build resilience and reframe our struggles as growth opportunities. A daily gratitude practice enables us to look past the difficulties in our lives and recognize the good things we have in front of us—blessings we might take for granted and would miss if they were taken away. Sharing your struggles with a resilient person can also help you look at your situation in a new light and move past it rather than becoming paralyzed by the problem.

Building resilience can help keep the stress of difficult situations from building up. Stress isn't good for mind, body, or spirit—and certainly not good for living the life of joy and intention that we desire.

One technique I use to build my resilience is to remind myself of my strength and how far I've come. List three difficult situations you have gotten through in the past.

How were you able to get through those situations? Describe how they were growth opportunities for you.

Try using the 5 x 5 rule. Ask yourself: Will this situation matter in five years? If not, give yourself five minutes to think about it, then move on. When could you have used this technique to save yourself the worry?

Who in your life is resilient? Why does this person come to mind? How can you learn from their example?

PRACTICING THE PAUSE

> Practice the pause. Pause before judging. Pause before assuming. Pause before accusing. Pause whenever you're about to react harshly and you'll avoid doing and saying things you'll later regret.
>
> —LORI DESCHENE

One of the most beneficial techniques I've found to help me deal with thousands of different personalities on a daily basis is to practice the pause. We can get so tied up in our day, with a million things going on, that we react immediately when something happens. This habit can lead to poor choices in words and actions, and cause hurt feelings and regret. By practicing the pause, we give ourselves time to respond in a way that aligns with our heart and values.

This technique can take some practice if you're a knee-jerk reactor by nature, but I promise it's worth it. You'll develop a better sense of self and a clearer understanding of what the other person meant. Tone can get lost so easily in emails and texts, and it can be difficult to discern someone's intended meaning on the initial read.

How much time we allow will depend on the situation, of course. For a face-to-face conversation, counting to 10 while breathing deeply is a good start. You may want to sleep on an email or text, and then respond when you've had a chance to clearly think it through. Putting your hand over your heart can be helpful to remind you of the importance of your response.

Before responding in a sticky situation, ask yourself: "Does it need to be said? Do *I* need to say it? Do I need to say it *now*?" Describe how this technique could have helped you in the past.

Think of a time when someone interpreted your tone in a way you didn't intend. What happened? How could you have prevented it?

Write down five ways you can remind yourself to pause, such as taking a few cleansing breaths, counting to 10, and taking a step back.

What other situations in your life would benefit from you pausing before responding?

ESTABLISHING A REGULAR GRATITUDE PRACTICE

I am determined to live with an attitude of gratitude to build my resilience and bring more positive things into my life. Gratitude puts my entire life into perspective.

My daily gratitude practice is my single most powerful tool for living with wholehearted joy and intention. By reminding ourselves of the good we have in our lives, we can actually rewire our brains, which naturally default to a negative mindset.

Establishing and maintaining a regular gratitude practice is essential to our growth and helps us keep our lives in perspective. Studies have shown that people who practice gratitude have a more positive outlook on life, better sleep, and lower blood pressure. They also build stronger relationships with others and have more resilience. You definitely want this powerful punch in your daily routine.

The primary purpose of my Facebook community is to help people who live with chronic physical or emotional pain use gratitude as a tool for living a life of joy, fulfillment, and intention. By celebrating our blessings with each other rather than focusing on our struggles, we can strengthen our own feelings of appreciation while highlighting what *isn't* going wrong in our lives.

You can use all kinds of methods to incorporate more gratitude into your life. Keeping a gratitude journal or joining a gratitude community can bring enormous benefits and serve as an important reminder to savor your blessings.

Often we don't appreciate what we have until it's gone. This week, try to focus on what's in front of you. What have you lost that you wish you could get back?

How might you look at your life through the lens of abundance and gratitude? Perhaps find a gratitude buddy and commit to exchanging a daily text or email, sharing what you're grateful for.

Being mindful and savoring our experiences as we have them will help us reframe how we view them. What are some ways you can slow down this week?

Gratitude journaling or joining a gratitude group on social media can help you keep a daily practice. Think of ways you can incorporate gratitude into your day, and write down your thoughts.

REMINDING YOURSELF HOW FAR YOU'VE COME

You are your best thing.

—TONI MORRISON

It can be easy to become so hyper-focused on our desired end result that we forget to enjoy the process and appreciate how far we've come. Looking back without regret can serve as a reminder of what we've already overcome and boost our journey toward a life that sets our soul on fire.

Being able to objectively look back at our past without judgment, appreciate the lessons we've learned along the way, and celebrate what we've accomplished is an important part of the process toward living a life of wholehearted joy and intention. Each setback is an opportunity for a comeback, and being able to reframe mistakes as lessons will help us embody a growth mindset.

Ruminating on the past is counterproductive to moving forward; we can't walk the path toward the life we want if our head is constantly looking back. If you find yourself drifting into the future or staying stuck in the past, stop what you're doing, put your hand over your heart, close your eyes, and take three deep inhalations and exhalations. Checking in with yourself in this way will allow you to stay more mindful and ready to move ahead throughout the day.

Everyone has setbacks along their journey, and it's natural to think of them as mistakes. Think of a past setback you regret, and describe how you could reframe it as a lesson.

Journaling my journey and looking at old pictures of myself are great motivators to keep me moving forward. What tool(s) could you use to remind yourself how far you've come?

Write down any regrets you can think of, then crumple them up and throw them away. Remind yourself that they no longer serve you. Describe how you feel afterward.

How would your best friend or someone who loves you describe your journey so far? Do you agree with this assessment? Why or why not?

ENDING EACH DAY ON A POSITIVE

I can enrich my life and move forward with confidence and intention by focusing on the positive things that happen throughout my day.

Ending your day on a positive note helps reduce stress and anxiety, and keeps you on track to living your best intentional life. Incorporating a gratitude practice into our lives rewires our brains to see the positive. By focusing on gratitude and what's going well, you can dilute the negative instances and put your day into perspective. This approach will help you move forward with focus and joy toward a bright tomorrow.

In my community, at the end of every day, we have a "three good things" post. Members post three things they did well that day. The focus is not on major accomplishments, but rather recognizing things we may not normally view as a win. It prompts us to look at our lives in a more positive light, which increases our optimism, boosts our joy, and allows us to be excited in our journey instead of getting stuck on the few bad things that may happen along the way.

If you make it a daily practice, you'll start to see positive results in your mood and focus, as well as a boost in your resilience.

Each day brings personal victories that we may not recognize; for example, sometimes simply taking a shower or returning a phone call is a win. List three things you accomplished today that you can celebrate.

Your productivity can change significantly depending on whether you're in a good headspace or a bad one. Describe these differences as they apply to you.

Give an example of how having a positive attitude at the end of your day made you see a situation differently. Why do you think that is? Try to think of specifics.

Write about how you can end each day with a positive, and make it a daily practice. For example, at bedtime, write down three good things you did that day.

ENCOURAGING OTHERS

I don't need to see myself as being in competition with anyone to curate the life I desire. There is enough room for everyone to shine, and I will do my part to share the light.

Throughout our lives, we're fed messages such as "every man for himself" and "survival of the fittest." Although we do need to take care of ourselves first and should aim to avoid putting everyone else's needs before our own, we can find enormous delight and gifts by encouraging others to succeed and embracing the mindset that there's room for everybody to shine.

There's no doubt we live in a competitive world. By nature, we want to be the best at what we do. When you find a group of like-minded people you strive to emulate, you can encourage them and promote their success while still working toward your own. Engaging in healthy competition—the kind that inspires us and leads to improvement—and being fueled by someone else's success are beneficial, but sometimes competing can distract us to the point where we lose sight of our primary focus.

You'll find that the more you promote and encourage others, the more they'll do the same for you. Pivoting from a life of mindlessness to a life of mindfulness requires giving and receiving. By offering your support to others, you can hold your head high while still walking toward the light yourself. It's a win-win for everyone!

Describe a time when you lost your way because you were overly competitive or became preoccupied with comparing yourself to someone else.

How could you have shifted this focus while still working toward your intention?

Think of a time when someone promoted or encouraged you. How did it make you feel? Why?

How can you harness your light and pass it on? Sharing others' achievements through your social media and recommending them to others will give them a boost while your own light shines.

DON'T TAKE THINGS PERSONALLY

I have a beautiful soul and live my life with wholehearted intention. The only opinion that matters is the opinion I have of myself, and I know I am worthy and valuable in this life.

One of my favorite personal-development books is *The Four Agreements* by Don Miguel Ruiz. He offers four rules based on ancient Toltec wisdom and urges the reader to use them as a way to live their best life.

One of these agreements is to not take anything personally. It took me quite a while to break free from this type of thinking, but when I did, I started living with much more freedom. I was no longer bound by my emotions. I could finally move forward with my head held high rather than ruminating over others' insensitive or unkind comments.

It can be difficult to avoid getting caught up in others' opinions of us; after all, we're deeply feeling humans. But whatever is done or said to you has nothing to do with you, and everything to do with the other person. When you live your best, most intentional life, you'll walk with your head high and have nothing to fear. You know your own value and what you have to offer because you're living a wholehearted and mindful life of authenticity.

Valuing and believing in ourselves begins with the understanding that whatever anyone thinks of us is none of our business.

Allowing the actions or words of another to bother us is an admission that we believe what they say to be true. Describe a time when someone's words hurt you deeply.

How would your reaction to those words have been different if you hadn't taken them personally?

Write a positive mantra or affirmation you can repeat to yourself when someone hurts you (such as "What others think of me is none of my business").

Keep this affirmation in your sacred space to remind yourself daily of why you're worthy of love and valuable to the world. How do you feel after you repeat it?

MINDFULNESS

Mindfulness is a way of befriending ourselves
and our experience.

—JON KABAT-ZINN

When we hear the word *mindfulness*, meditation often comes to mind. Mindfulness meditation has surged in popularity over the past decade—and for good reason, as it helps us slow down and focus on the moment.

But mindfulness by definition doesn't mean meditation. According to the *Oxford Dictionary*, mindfulness is "the quality or state of being conscious or aware of something." In other words, being mindful means slowing down, not doing too many things at once, and increasing our awareness of what's going on in this very moment. Basically, it means to live with intention.

By staying in the moment, we can reduce anxiety about the future. Being mindful takes away our need to continually rush to the next thing, giving us the ability to do one thing at a time and do it well. We're all in.

Find what keeps you engaged and in the moment, whether writing letters, meditating, adult coloring, or laughing with a friend. Meditation or intentional breathwork have enormous health benefits, both physical and mental. Figure out what works for you, and add it to your tool kit to use whenever you need it.

Practicing mindfulness involves activities that keep us engaged and in the now. What activity do you give of yourself 100 percent? How does it help you forget about the outside world?

How can you add this interest to your regular routine? What kind of adjustments can you make to allow for it?

Try slowing your breathing for a few minutes. Relax your jaw and shoulders. Describe the difference in how you feel afterward and what you enjoyed or found challenging.

How can meditation or deep breathing add value to your life? What kind of commitment are you willing to make to add it to your day?

EMBRACING YOUR AUTHENTIC SELF

I love my authentic self in all my imperfect ways. I will strive for progress and learning instead of aiming for perfection, and I will live each moment with courage and vulnerability.

In this age of social media, where so much appears perfect, it can be easy to get caught up in the desire to make ourselves and our lives appear to be something they're not. On social media posts, we see people's carefully curated highlight reels. Keeping this fact in mind will help us recognize the value in being our authentic selves.

Perfection is a myth—and even if there were such a thing, what a boring existence it would be! I am drawn to the klutzes in life: the people who snort when they laugh, whose houses are not picture-perfect but look lived in, who admit their mistakes and grow from them. A quest for perfection can prevent us from moving forward with confidence and courage.

Our authentic selves are beautiful and what our true friends see. They like us for who we are. When we love ourselves and embrace a mindset of "progress, not perfection," we allow ourselves to be the perfectly imperfect humans we are.

Show the true you in all your vulnerability. You are magnificent in all your messy authenticity, and you have nobody to impress but yourself. Celebrate you, and embrace your inner dork.

We can become paralyzed by our quest toward (nonexistent) perfection. Has this been an issue for you, or are you able to be yourself easily? Why do you think this is?

What are some imperfections that others find endearing about you?

I gravitate toward people who share their true selves. How do you feel when others share their imperfect selves? Does it drive you away, or do you find it refreshing and comforting? Why?

Write yourself a love letter, highlighting your quirks and imperfections. Ask your family and friends to contribute. Read this letter when you feel caught up in the pursuit of perfection.

MAKING YOUR BED

I can gift myself my first win of the day by taking a few minutes to make my bed. A made bed signifies a productive and intentional life.

Each morning, without fail, I make my bed. I started this practice many years ago and consider it a vital jump-start to my day. I frequently recommend it to members of my community who are looking for tips on living an intentional life.

How can something as mundane as making your bed be beneficial? You'd be surprised! First, it sends our brain a signal that we're done with bed for the day. It also gives us an easy early sense of accomplishment, which is a fantastic start to the day because it allows us to hit the ground running with intention. Making the bed takes only a few minutes, but its enormous psychological benefits will pay off in the long run.

Besides gifting you with that first accomplishment of the day, making your bed helps you maintain the clutter-free environment that we aim for to reduce stress. And who doesn't prefer to climb into a made bed each night? It's a much more pleasurable experience and helps us settle into a more peaceful sleep—another important aspect of our wellness.

Describe your current bed-making habit. Then make a list of five things you'd like to accomplish early in the day.

You may not realize it, but an unmade bed can bother you subconsciously and affect your mood. What are three things you can do to keep your home tidy?

How does an unmade bed or a sink full of dishes, for example, affect your daily mindset? Why do you think that is?

Creating a sacred space where we sleep can be so beneficial to our overall mood. How can you make your bed more inviting (such as buying a new pillow or washing your sheets more often)?

FOSTERING CREATIVITY

Creativity is inventing, experimenting, growing, taking risks, breaking rules, making mistakes, and having fun.

—MARY LOU COOK

Adding creativity to our lives is not only fun, but also rewards us with a number of benefits. Many studies over the past decade have shown that creativity is actually a wellness practice, and it can be just as important to our health as proper nutrition, exercise, and meditation. It can even help prevent cognitive decline.

Being engaged in something creative is a very mindful process. When I'm playing with my watercolors, writing, or even making graphics for my group, I'm fully engaged and in the moment as the creative side of my brain takes over. There's no room for my mind to wander to a place of anxiety, and I experience each moment with intention.

You don't have to be artistic to be creative. Incorporating creativity into your day is a form of self-care and can be very grounding. As children, we were free with our creativity, not caring so much about the result being good enough. According to art therapist and best-selling author Lacy Mucklow, "Doing something creative that you enjoy, no matter what your skill level, is something that provides a positive mindset and can be helpful both as a regular self-care practice as well as a way of self-soothing when you've had a particularly rough day."

Think about the less inhibited creativity you likely had as a child. How can you return to that state? Is creativity something that comes easily for you? Why or why not?

What types of creative activities did you enjoy as a child? Maybe you loved painting, making latch hook rugs (I did!), or writing poetry. How has that shifted in adulthood?

How might you embrace the creative process and drop the fear that something won't be "good enough"? (You're not displaying your work in a gallery!) How can you incorporate more creativity into your day?

I don't consider myself artistic, yet I love cooking, and my creative juices flow through that outlet. Name a few ways you're creative that perhaps you've never considered.

MOVING YOUR BODY

If you can't fly, run; if you can't run, walk; if you can't walk, crawl; but by all means keep moving.

—DR. MARTIN LUTHER KING JR.

Exercise is one of those words that causes people to either tense up or get excited. People who exercise regularly swear by it and get a high from the good feelings it produces. Studies show that those who exercise tend to have better mental health because it reduces anxiety and depression and boosts self-esteem and cognitive function. Moving our bodies also provides us with many physical benefits.

Not everyone is capable of rigorous exercise each day, and exercise is not one-size-fits-all because people have a wide range of physical abilities. It's up to you to determine what you can realistically do to reap the benefits of exercise. It also helps if exercise involves something you enjoy because you're more likely to stick with it.

We can move our bodies in many different ways that aren't necessarily rigorous. If you can walk, finding a walking partner, preferably someone in your circle of friends or family, will give you both the social and physical benefits of exercise. Chair yoga is a wonderful way to stretch your muscles without overexerting; countless YouTube videos show various techniques to get you moving without leaving your chair.

Stretching throughout the day, finding a walking partner, and doing qigong or yoga are all wonderful ways to get moving. How can you incorporate enjoyable movement into your life?

What action steps can you take to stay committed to movement? Deciding on a time and adding it to your daily schedule can keep you on track.

When you're moving or stretching in some way, how does your physical self feel afterward? List three health benefits you experience when you incorporate exercise into your day.

In what ways does movement improve your mood? Be as specific as you can.

PAMPERING YOURSELF

*Love yourself first and everything else falls into line.
You really have to love yourself to get anything done in
this world.*

—LUCILLE BALL

Self-care includes treating ourselves on occasion. Getting frequent massages or going to luxurious spas may not be a possibility for most of us on a regular basis, but we can do many things to feel pampered and practice the self-love we all deserve.

You can do small things for yourself that will enable you to feel cared for. Light a candle, play some relaxing music, meditate, sleep in late once in a while, take a bubble bath, or give yourself a facial. None of these things requires much time or money—you only need to make the time in your schedule.

Self-care and pampering are not selfish; they are vital. To be good for anyone else, we must first take care of ourselves. If you can, set aside money each month for a special day. Go by yourself to a movie, splurge on your favorite takeout food, or spend some time out in the sun with a good book.

The rewards you reap from focusing on yourself will help you stay mindful, motivated, and on track to the life of intention you desire and deserve.

What kind of pampering or self-care do you give yourself? Do you feel it's enough? Is there some kind of self-care approach you'd like to try?

Describe a time when you pampered yourself. How did you feel afterward?

It's important to release feelings of guilt about treating yourself. List five ways you can pamper yourself, and include something you've always wanted to try. What can you do to make it happen?

Write yourself a special mantra to give yourself permission to treat yourself. (Some suggestions: "I am worthy of pampering" or "Pampering myself is self-care, not selfish.")

RANDOM ACTS OF KINDNESS

By sharing kindness toward others, I am doing my part to spread my light in the world and make it a better place.

A healthy gratitude practice involves not only feeling and expressing gratitude, but also passing it on and sharing it. Kindness, like smiling, laughing, and gratitude, is contagious: the more we share it and pay it forward, the happier we become. It's a win-win situation when we help others because we're also helping ourselves.

Letting someone go ahead of you in the checkout line, paying for the person behind you at the tollbooth, writing a thank-you note to someone who wouldn't expect it, saying a kind word to the boss or a worker who went out of their way to help you, or even simply smiling at a stranger can make someone's day when they least expect it.

I make it a point to commend people who provide me with good service. I often tell servers at restaurants, "You're very good at what you do." Baggers at the grocery store checkout are frequently overlooked, so I always thank them. Giving a big smile to someone you come in contact with can make their day better, in turn making yours better. I can't tell you how many times I've thanked service workers, and their faces just lit up. Paying kindness forward will reap amazing rewards.

Describe something kind you did for someone you didn't know. What made you do it, and how did you feel afterward? If you were able to see their reaction, what was it?

How do you practice random acts of kindness in your everyday life? Do you thank people freely? Do you hold the door open for the person behind you?

Identify an occasion when someone paid you kindness. How did it make you feel? Describe how you can pay forward this sort of kindness.

Think of three acts of service you could easily incorporate into your day. Make it a point this week to work toward acting on them.

DON'T OVERDO

> Moderation. Small helpings. Sample a little bit of everything.
> These are the secrets of happiness and good health.
>
> —JULIA CHILD

Too much of a good thing can be detrimental to achieving our goals. Too often, we get overly excited about a new project and go all in, only to find our enthusiasm waning because we went too fast. We become addicted to our actions, and although giving our intentions our full attention is exactly what we're aiming for, overdoing any activity doesn't pay off in the end because the quality of our work suffers.

I used to have a problem with overcommitting myself, and I'd suffer from burnout by the end of the process. I relished being known as the girl who did it all, which prompted me to say yes to nearly every request that came my way. Need something typed up? Sure! Organize that fundraiser? Absolutely! But as that burnout became increasingly frequent, I found myself crashing hard, which led to eating poorly and drinking too much.

Finding balance is a daily activity for me, and through my intentions, I'm aware of it and can focus on that sweet spot of a happy medium. Practicing moderation is an art. You'll discover that you're happier when you respect your abilities because you'll be able to give each activity your all and avoid spreading yourself too thin. Value yourself enough to know when to say when.

Working too much or volunteering for everything under the sun can catch up to us. What is an example of something you overdid in the past or continue to overdo today?

How difficult is it for you to say no to people? What has been your biggest challenge regarding saying yes to too many things and overcommitting?

How can you address the tendency to overdo? How would your life and mindset improve if you cut some excess activity from your schedule?

Saying no can be challenging. Write yourself an affirmation that will help you recognize that saying no doesn't require an explanation (e.g., "I will carefully think before I commit").

WATERING AND FEEDING OURSELVES

I feel great when I treat my body with gentle care and respect myself by eating and drinking mindfully and nutritiously. I stop when I feel full, so I don't overindulge.

Just as a garden grows best with the right nutrients, our bodies perform best when we eat a healthy, balanced diet. Eating and drinking poorly causes a host of problems and can affect our physical, emotional, and mental well-being.

Diets consisting mostly of junky food with empty calories and sugary drinks will cause us to feel run-down and crash in the middle of the day. A poor diet can also cause health and weight issues that affect our self-esteem and confidence. By focusing on eating high-nutrient foods and staying hydrated, we can ensure peak performance and have more energy to keep us going longer and with more vigor.

Through talking to your physician and listening to your body, you can determine what your optimal diet is. Eating mindfully can prevent us from overeating. I love using chopsticks because they help me slow down, allowing me to better determine when I'm full. Take time to really chew your food, and don't rush.

Staying hydrated is also very important; making sure we get enough water helps us stay healthy. Determine how much water you should be drinking, and set an intention to reach that daily goal.

How we eat plays a large part in how we get through our day. What are your current eating habits, and where would you like to see improvement? Be specific.

How can you make it easier on yourself to stick to a well-balanced and nutritious diet? (Would prepping meals ahead of time help?)

Write a meal plan for this week and do your best to stick to it. What difference do you see in your mood and performance depending on what you eat?

How much water do you drink each day? If you feel you need improvement, a special bottle with a fill line can help you keep track.

DON'T COMPARE

Comparison is the thief of joy.

—ANONYMOUS

In this age of social media, we're inundated with the highlight reels of those we follow. We see the best of everyone's lives, which can leave us feeling inadequate, as though we're not enough or we're not doing enough. It's easy to have FOMO (fear of missing out) after a long social media session, and we may make unhealthy comparisons between ourselves and others.

Living our best life of intention might involve us modeling our path with inspiration from someone we admire, but getting caught up in comparing ourselves to anyone else can be paralyzing. It's why success in our daily endeavors depends on working toward being content with our own path and losing our natural tendency to compare ourselves with others.

A lot of the tools we work on in this book can help. A solid gratitude practice helps us embrace the abundance we already have in our lives. Writing down our strengths and reciting affirmations daily will help remind us of why we're good enough as we are. Limiting the time we spend on social media is a smart move because comparison really is the thief of joy. But we can stop it by walking our path of intention.

If you have FOMO or feel anxious after scrolling on social media, how can you reduce your exposure? Can you unfollow certain accounts?

When something good happens to someone you care about, what is your initial reaction? Do you feel envious or are you happy for them? Why do you think that is?

Remembering that there's room for everyone to shine and that authenticity is a beautiful part of who you are can reduce feelings of inadequacy and jealousy. Write down five things that make you amazing.

Sticking to a regular gratitude practice and focusing on what we have versus what we lack is important in reducing our need to compare. What are you grateful for today?

DETOXING FROM TOXICITY

I value my life's goals and walk toward a positive and mindful life. I will not allow toxic people to hold me back and will exercise self-care by reducing my exposure to them.

Toxicity can prevent us from living our best life. We're bombarded with toxic information, including news and ugly posts on social media. We also may encounter people who seem toxic and don't make us feel our best. They may be negative people who complain constantly, with no solutions offered.

To keep our eyes on the prize, we need to release toxic news and people from our lives. You can ease out so-called friends who make you feel small, don't support you, or bring nothing valuable to your life. This practice is optimal self-care and is necessary for you to stay focused on your own positive life of intention.

Sometimes the toxic people in our lives are family members, and we can't remove them. If you are in this situation, try to limit your exposure as much as possible. If you have a toxic encounter, try to detox by doing a short mindfulness breathing practice and recentering your thoughts.

Reduce news by directing your attention elsewhere and unsubscribing from social media accounts and channels that don't bring you positive energy. Unfollowing toxic people on social media will allow you to remain friends with them (if needed) while freeing you from exposure to their negative comments.

Where in your life do you feel toxicity seeping in? If it involves people you see regularly, list them and note why they are in your life. How might you change the situation?

How can you limit exposure to people who don't strive to live a positive life? If you can't remove toxic people from your life, set a time limit on how long you spend with them and stick to it.

Pay close attention to your day, and determine when and how toxic news or posts get to you. What can you do to remove them, or at least most of them? (Unsubscribing is your friend!)

Joining positive groups online and meditating are great ways to reduce toxic negativity and enhance your health. What other tools do you have that can help you live your most positive life?

DOING SERVICE

The unselfish effort to bring cheer to others will be the beginning of a happier life for ourselves.

—HELEN KELLER

Living a life of meaning involves being as well-rounded as possible. A well-rounded life means getting outside ourselves and helping others while also living mindfully and focusing on our personal needs and goals. Volunteering and doing service for others is a win-win for our best life.

Giving of ourselves in some form adds meaning to our lives. Service work feels good, and when you're helping a person or a cause you're passionate about, the work not only is rewarding but also helps your self-esteem. Some people devote their lives to service, while others add it in here and there as they're able.

While being careful not to overcommit and spread ourselves too thin, giving a little bit of ourselves each day reduces our stress and boosts our mood. Knowing you can make a difference, no matter how much time you can devote, brings endless gifts that enable us to live with more purpose. Take a look at your schedule and your life's intention to determine where you can be of most use. We all have causes that are near and dear to us.

Take a look at your goals and your daily schedule. Where can you add helping others without feeling overwhelmed? Could you commit to volunteering once a month?

How have you volunteered or given of yourself in the past? Perhaps you've been a home-room parent, or you made a meal for a friend or neighbor going through a difficult time.

List some charities that have meaning for you. How can you contribute your efforts to the cause? Organizations' websites often have information about how you can help.

When you're doing service for others, how do you feel emotionally? Why do you think that is?

CONNECTING WITH NATURE/ GROUNDING

I fill my soul and gift myself with optimal health by connecting with nature and spending time outdoors.

Spending time in nature offers many health benefits. Taking a walk outside can bring us the body movement we need while we soak in the abundance of nature's beauty, and you can enjoy nature in many ways.

Working in the garden, standing outside barefoot, lying on the ground, and even hugging a tree are ways to connect with nature. These are all forms of grounding, a therapeutic technique that many experts promote. The benefits include reducing inflammation, cardiovascular disease, muscle damage, and even chronic pain. Grounding is also said to improve sleep and to reduce anxiety and depression. The sun provides us with vitamin D, which has its own set of health benefits that improve our mood.

I love growing heirloom tomatoes and various herbs in my outdoor garden in the summer. Getting my hands in the dirt (I call it "dirt therapy"), watching my plants sprout from seed and grow, and eventually harvesting them provides me with nourishment and constitute a great mindfulness practice. Being connected to the earth allows us to put our troubles into perspective. Fresh air can help us refocus, bring us into the here and now, and get us back on track toward intention and awareness.

Connecting with nature helps us become more mindful, getting us out of our own heads when we need to. What are some ways you currently connect with nature?

Common experiences of being at one with nature include being invigorated, having less anxiety, and feeling connected with the universe. What kinds of emotions come up when you're out in nature?

Grounding (or earthing) is an intentional act of connecting ourselves with the earth. How can you incorporate dirt therapy or grounding into your daily intentions? Try a few activities this week and journal how you feel afterward. Do you feel different depending on what you're doing?

Describe a time when you felt the most connected to the earth and your surroundings.

SELF-COMPASSION

I deserve the love, compassion, and patience I give so freely to others. I am in love with myself and am worthy of my own support and tenderness.

Many of us have never learned to have compassion for ourselves, yet it's essential to living our best life. For some, treating others with love and tenderness comes easily. We can have great patience with others when they're in a bad space, but we often don't treat ourselves the same way. Setting a different standard for ourselves is not only unfair to us, but also can lead to resentment.

The way you treat and speak to yourself is more important than you may realize. Using language such as "I *should* be able to do this" or losing your temper with yourself may seem harmless, but we believe everything we tell ourselves—and we need to take our self-talk seriously.

By flipping the script and treating ourselves with the same TLC we give others, we're cutting ourselves some much-needed slack. Falling in love with yourself and becoming your own best friend will help you succeed because you're giving yourself that important support you give others.

You are human. There's no reason to expect more of yourself than you would of your best friend. If you don't have your own back, how can anyone else? You are worthy of your own love and compassion.

Through stressful times, it's easy to lose our temper and lash out at ourselves. Describe a time you've done so and how you felt afterward.

How could you have approached that situation differently? List a couple of ways.

When you root yourself in self-love, you experience more in life because you allow yourself to make mistakes. How has a past "stupid mistake" turned out to be for the best?

An affirmation or mantra can remind you to be your own BFF. Write one to yourself based on self-compassion and love. It can be a few sentences if needed. Place it somewhere visible.

SMILING

Let your smile change the world, but don't let the world change your smile.

—CONNOR FRANTA

In a previous week, we focused on the lighter side of life and bringing laughter into each day. The act of smiling offers just as many overall benefits.

Many think of smiling as an involuntary response to things that bring us joy or make us laugh, but it can also be a choice that adds even more happiness to our lives. Whether your smile is organic or forced, you can still reap the many benefits for your body, mind, and mood.

Studies show that people in stressful situations have lower blood pressure and a better response to emotional stress when they smile, regardless of whether the smile comes naturally. Putting a half-smile on your face when your mood needs a boost is very effective in reducing stress and anxiety.

If it feels odd to smile for no reason, try holding a straw or a chopstick horizontally between your lips, producing a fake smile. This tactic works, and it's a quick and simple way to boost your mood.

Smiling also draws more people to us and is contagious, creating a beautiful and endless cycle of joy.

Describe a time when you were out in public and had to stop to ask someone for directions. How did you decide whom to approach? Did you seek out someone who was smiling?

Do you think others consider you to be approachable? Why do you suppose that is?

How can you remind yourself to smile more often? How can smiling more help you in your everyday life, such as when you're feeling stressed?

If smiling doesn't necessarily come easily to you, try the chopstick trick on page 151. How does this practice change your mood?

REST AND SLEEP

Sleep time is sacred and is vital for me to live a happy and healthy life. I make it a priority as a gift to myself.

Getting adequate sleep is important for our physical and mental health. So many of us are sleep deprived, which can lead to a host of health issues. Most adults need at least seven hours of sleep each night to keep our minds and bodies healthy.

When we get enough good-quality sleep, we are less likely to get sick, we deal with stress better, and we lower our risk for serious health problems, such as heart issues, diabetes, and obesity. Sleep also helps us perform optimally, maintain a good mood, and make better decisions.

Keeping a regular sleep routine is important. Turning off electronic devices and making your bed a no-work zone will help you relax at bedtime. Engaging in regular exercise and spending time outdoors will also help you fall asleep more easily. Keeping a sleep diary can help you see how much sleep you need, and many phone apps are available to help you track your sleep habits.

Sleep is essential for us to live mindfully, clearly, and with intention. It improves our relationships with others and boosts our confidence levels. We need to treat it as a priority, not an afterthought, to be our best self.

Creating a soothing, comfortable sleeping environment can be a big help in making sure we sleep soundly. What can you do to provide yourself with a sleeping oasis?

Take notes about your sleep this week. Note patterns or areas where you can improve (e.g., the time you go to bed each night).

How does lack of sleep affect you? Perhaps it takes a toll on your productivity or your mood. When has sleeping poorly had an impact on your day? How did you handle it?

What do you do when you can't sleep? Thinking of things you're grateful for, starting with each letter of the alphabet, is a great alternative to counting sheep.

A FINAL WORD

Congratulations! You've given yourself the gift of these 52 weeks, and you now hold these special tools that will set your soul on fire and help you fall deeply in love with your life. You're flipping the script of your story and changing it to read the way you want it to read: as a story that brings you infinite joy and wholehearted fulfillment. It may not have been easy; digging deep into ourselves can be difficult. But you suited up and showed up, and now you're applying these new strategies to live deliberately and positively. Your willingness to complete this journal has turned your blank canvas into a colorful masterpiece!

You may have completed this journal, but your work is not done. Use what you've learned about yourself to tweak each day to suit your needs. Treat yourself and your life with the respect they deserve. Walk forward with your head held high, knowing you deserve a life of happiness and meaning. Keep an open mind and make adjustments when needed, but stick to your tools. Refer to this journal often, and remind yourself of where you were—then catapult yourself to where you envision going!

Your superpower burns inside you, ready to be shared with the world. Your dreams are within reach. With this new life of intention, your eyes are open to enjoying each moment in all its splendor. By sticking to your intentions and keeping your eyes on the prize, you'll exude a glorious light of courage and gratitude that others will gravitate toward. Pass it on.

Most important, continue this path for *you*. You shine like a diamond, and nothing is standing in your way. Your life is calling you *right now*. It's time for you to respond with an enthusiastic "I'm here! I'm ready!"

You've got this.

RESOURCES

ONLINE RESOURCES

Action for Happiness

ActionForHappiness.org

> Action for Happiness is a movement of people committed to building a happier and more caring society.

Calm

Calm.com

> This app is great for sleep, meditation, relaxation, and mindfulness.

Gratitude Addict

GratitudeAddict.com

> This site and community offers support and guidance for those looking to live a more purposeful life with joy, intention, and gratitude even through life's ups and downs.

Tiny Buddha

TinyBuddha.com

> This site offers simple wisdom and teaches new ways to apply it to our complex lives.

PRINT RESOURCES

Brown, Brené. *The Gifts of Imperfection: Let Go of Who You Think You're Supposed to Be and Embrace Who You Are*. Center City, MN: Hazelden Publishing, 2010.

García, Héctor, and Francesc Miralles. *Ikigai: The Japanese Secret to a Long and Happy Life*. New York: Penguin Books, 2017.

Graham, Linda. *Resilience: Powerful Practices for Bouncing Back from Disappointment, Difficulty, and Even Disaster*. Novato, CA: New World Library, 2018.

Hay, Louise. *You Can Heal Your Life*. New York: Hay House, 1984.

Nelson, Kristi. *Wake Up Grateful: The Transformative Practice of Taking Nothing for Granted*. North Adams, MA: Storey Publishing, 2020.

Ruiz, Don Miguel. *The Four Agreements: A Practical Guide to Personal Freedom*. San Rafael, CA: Amber-Allen Publishing, 1997.

Sincero, Jen. *You Are a Badass: How to Stop Doubting Your Greatness and Start Living an Awesome Life*. Philadelphia, PA: Running Press, 2013.

REFERENCES

Cascio, Christopher N., Matthew Brook O'Donnell, et al. "Self-Affirmation Activates Brain Systems Associated with Self-Related Processing and Reward and Is Reinforced by Future Orientation." *Social Cognitive and Affective Neuroscience* 11, no. 4 (2015): 621–29. DOI.org/10.1093/scan/nsv136.

Chevalier, Gaétan. "The Effect of Grounding the Human Body on Mood." *Psychological Reports* 116, no. 2 (April 2015): 534–42. DOI.org/10.2466/06.PR0.116k21w5.

Dean, Jeremy. *Making Habits, Breaking Habits: Why We Do Things, Why We Don't, and How to Make Any Change Stick.* Boston, MA: Da Capo Lifelong Books, 2013.

Graff, Frank. "How Many Daily Decisions Do We Make?" UNC-TV Science. February 7, 2018. Science.UNCTV.org/content/reportersblog/choices.

Hamilton, Jon. "Think You're Multitasking? Think Again." NPR. October 2, 2008. NPR.org/templates/story/story.php?storyId=95256794.

Harvard Health Publishing. "Giving Thanks Can Make You Happier." August 14, 2021. Health.Harvard.edu/healthbeat/giving-thanks-can-make-you-happier.

"How Long Does It Take to Form a Habit?" UCL News, November 15, 2018. UCL.ac.uk/news/2009/aug/how-long-does-it-take-form-habit.

Kraft, Tara L., and Sarah D. Pressman. "Grin and Bear It: The Influence of Manipulated Facial Expression on the Stress Response." *Psychological Science* 23, no. 11 (2012).

Sharma, Ashish, Vishal Madaan, and Frederick D. Petty. "Exercise for Mental Health." *The Primary Care Companion to the Journal of Clinical Psychiatry* 8, no. 2 (2006): 106. NCBI.NLM.NIH.gov/pmc/articles/PMC1470658.

U.S. Department of Health and Human Services. "Your Guide to Healthy Sleep." September 2011. NHLBI.NIH.gov/files/docs/public/sleep/healthysleepfs.pdf.

ACKNOWLEDGMENTS

This book is for my parents, who never let me go a minute in this life without knowing I was loved and cherished. For Riley and Jake, who never gave up on me and trusted I would continue on the right path with the best intentions. For Jumby, Eric, and the Traveling Circus for your endless support. For Dr. Bruce Singer, who showed me where the path was, and for all the members of Attitude of Gratitude with Chronic Pain for reminding me daily to keep walking toward a life of beautiful intention. For Aimee, who showed me how to live each day as if it were my last. And, as always, for my husband, Rob, who gifts me with the best life possible and all the love and support in the world. I am forever grateful.

ABOUT THE AUTHOR

 Lauren Blanchard Zalewski is a writer, speaker, and passionate champion of all things gratitude. She is also a self-diagnosed gratitude addict—hence her blog name, GratitudeAddict.com.

She is the founder of the Facebook group Attitude of Gratitude with Chronic Pain, and she hosts the weekly live broadcast "Gratefully Living the Chronic Life," which streams on both Facebook Live and YouTube. She is also the author of *5-Minute Gratitude Journal for Teen Boys*.

Lauren is a student of the human experience. Her passion and life's work is spreading the message that gratitude and living with intention are the ultimate tools for resilience, hope, and joy, even through the most difficult circumstances. She has lived with chronic pain and illness for more than 20 years, and her work has helped thousands of others who struggle with the effects of chronic physical and emotional conditions to find purpose, happiness, and intention in their lives.

The mother of two grown children, Lauren lives in Hunterdon County, New Jersey, with her husband, Rob.

Follow her at GratitudeAddict.com.